From Orphan to Queen

Shifting From Lack and Survival Into Divine Purpose and Royalty

Gail Wright-Barron

Edited by
Nicole Queen

Vision Publishing House
support@vision-publishinghouse.com
www.vision-publishinghouse.com

ISBN: 979-8-9933667-0-8 (print)
LCCN: 2025921819

This book is established to provide information and inspiration to all readers. It is designed with the understanding that the author is not engaged to render any psychological, legal, or any other kind of professional advice. The content is the sole expression of the author. The author is not liable for any physical, psychological, emotional, financial, or commercial damages, including, but not limited to special, incidental, consequential, or other damages. All readers are responsible for their own choices, actions, and results.

This workbook is dedicated to my B.A.P.S. (Black American Princesses):
my daughters, Erica Michelle Wright and Tiera Enjoli Barron,
and my nieces, Denise Lynette Bryant-Cook and Monica Sherese Bryant.

I love you with all my heart.
Grow! Glow! and Go!

Inspired By Lessie R. Hill-Wright

"Favor is deceitful, and beauty is vain, but a woman who feareth the Lord shall be praised."

— Proverbs 31:30

Contents

Welcome!

Although this workbook is written with women in mind, I believe it holds value for men, as well. I'm writing the workbook I wish I had when I needed guidance the most. My prayer is that you will take this journey with me, with an open heart and a willing spirit.

Together, we will uncover hidden treasures within you and unlock doors to greater opportunities, deeper purpose, and divine destiny. Someone is assigned to your voice, and they are waiting to hear it.

Your path will not be without struggles, distractions, setbacks, or disappointments. But with faith in God and hard work, you will be victorious.

"Now faith is the substance of things hoped for, the evidence of things not seen...
And without faith it is impossible to please God..."

— Hebrews 11:1, 6

Part One

Identity

Discovering Who You Are in God

Before you can walk in your calling, you must know who you are and whose you are. Identity is not defined by labels, circumstances, or family history—it is shaped by God's design and destiny. Just as Esther's name carried prophetic meaning, your name and story reveal purpose that goes deeper than you may realize. This section invites you to embrace the truth of your identity in Christ.

"Before I formed you in the womb I knew you, before you were born I set you apart." — Jeremiah 1:5

Chapter 1
What's in a Name?

A title serves as a formal distinction or denotes rank, authority, or profession. For example, "Doctor" or "Captain" can signal the position or job of an individual. It can signify respect or importance. On the other hand, a name is a specific word or set of words by which a person, place, or thing is identified, such as "Gail" or "Philadelphia." It's an identifier.

When I was born, my name was chosen: *Gail*—meaning "My father rejoices," "Joyful," "Cheerful," "Gives joy." I didn't realize it then, but this name wasn't just a label. It was a prophetic declaration. The meaning of my name speaks to creativity grounded in practicality. It's not just about having ideas; it's about bringing them to life. *Strong Gail*—a strong wind of force. My father once told me, "Continue to be the battle axe that you are." At the time, I didn't understand. But now I see: my name was speaking to my future and destiny before I even knew what they were.

> *You are my battle axe and weapons of war...*
>
> — Jeremiah 51:20

I had to do some research and look that word up.

What is a battle axe? In the Bible, a battle axe is a physical weapon of war symbolizing divine power, strength, and judgment.

3

A good axe must be:

- Swift: ready to move at the command of its Master
- Sharp: effective, precise, and able to cut through resistance
- Strong: able to withstand pressure without breaking
- Powerful: carrying authority and weight in battle

God's battle axe is characterized by:

- Its sharpness through the Word of God (Hebrews 4:12)
- Its ability to cut through and destroy strongholds of darkness
- Its processing through fire to gain strength, durability, and shape
- The availability and commitment of the believer to serve as a willing, effective instrument

When you see yourself as God's battle axe, you realize that your life is not random. You have been shaped, sharpened, and set apart as His instrument of victory. And now I know that I am not random. My name is not random.

When I look back at my experiences and all that I have endured, I can clearly see how God was shaping me as His battle axe. He was sharpening me through trials, refining me through fire, and positioning me to cut through strongholds—not just for myself, but also for my family and for the mission He has entrusted to me. Every season of pain, every moment of struggle, and every test was not wasted. They were all part of God forging me into a willing and effective instrument in His hands.

Just like me, Esther's name told her story before she lived it. Esther was a Jew from the tribe of Benjamin who grew up as an exile in Persia. Her Persian name, *Esther*, means "star," derived from the root name of the goddess Ishtar. Her Hebrew name, *Hadassah*, means "myrtle," a branch symbolizing peace and thanksgiving—two things Esther ultimately brought to her people.

...you shall be called by a new name that the mouth of the Lord will give.

— Isaiah 62:2

She was an orphan, without father or mother, raised by her older cousin Mordecai as his own daughter. Though she was part of the remnant permitted to return to Jerusalem, she stayed in Persia—positioned by God for a purpose she could not yet see.

* * *

Chapter 1 Reflection

Personal Reflection

1. What does your name mean? Beyond a label, could it carry a message about your purpose or destiny?

_____

_____

_____

_____

_____

_____

_____

_____

2. Are there parts of yourself that have been silenced, overlooked, or unrecognized?

_____

_____

_____

_____

_____

_____

_____

_____

3. What does the image of a "battle axe" mean to you personally?

_____

_____

_____

_____

_____

_____

_____

_____

4. When you think about your own life, where can you see God sharpening or refining you through trials?

_____

_____

_____

_____

_____

_____

_____

_____

_____

_____

_____

_____

_____

_____

5. What strongholds have you had to cut through in your own journey (personally, within your family, or in your community)?

_____

_____

_____

_____

_____

_____

_____

_____

_____

_____

_____

_____

_____

6. How does knowing your name and identity are not random change the way you view your purpose?

_____
_____
_____
_____
_____
_____
_____
_____
_____
_____
_____
_____
_____
_____
_____
_____

7. In what ways do you feel God may be positioning you to serve as His "battle axe" in this season of your life?

_____
_____
_____
_____
_____
_____
_____
_____
_____
_____
_____
_____
_____
_____
_____

Scripture Meditation

Meditate on God's intimate knowledge of you. He named you, set you apart, and ordained your path. After spending time with God and meditating on the Word below, write down anything He reveals to you. Be open and honest, despite any vulnerabilities.

> *Before I formed you in the womb I knew you, before you were born I set you apart; I appointed you as a prophet to the nations.*
>
> — Jeremiah 1:5

_____

_____

_____

_____

_____

_____

_____

_____

Practical Action Step

Write down your full name and its meaning. Reflect on how your life has already fulfilled or demonstrated aspects of that meaning. Then, consider one step you can take this week to align more fully with the calling embedded in your name.

_____

_____

_____

_____

_____

_____

_____

Chapter 2
Does My Situation Dictate My Future?

You might not have had the life you desired, or what others would consider ideal, but you can always take your lemons and make lemonade. And if it's too tart, go ahead and add some sugar. Sweetness can still come from sour places.

A caterpillar doesn't look like much. But it must go through metamorphosis to become that beautiful butterfly. In the same way, your current form isn't the final version of who you are becoming. The pain, the pressure, and the process are all part of your metamorphosis.

Earlier in my life, I believed my limitations in fulfilling my destiny were tied to two major things:

- *My gender.* I grew up believing that because this was "a man's world," certain roles, dreams, and callings were frowned upon for women. That opposition created an inner struggle I didn't yet know how to overcome.

- *My health.* In December 2017, I suffered a stroke that paralyzed my right side— my dominant side. My independence, confidence, and mobility were all suddenly challenged.

On Thanksgiving of 2018, my family spent the holiday with my son in Eugene, Oregon. On Black Friday, while others shopped, I sat in a massage chair in the middle of the mall, letting the crowd pass me by. My husband was sitting nearby. Then, it happened.

A complete stranger walked up to me and asked, "Can I say something to you?" I said, "Yes." My husband noticed and came closer. The man looked me straight in the eye and said,

"God said that what He told you to do has nothing to do with your disability." Tears welled up. He, then asked my husband for permission to pray for me right there in the middle of the mall.

That was the day I realized: God's calling is not restricted by my gender, my health, or my circumstances. His plan for me didn't shrink when my body faced challenges. It didn't expire when culture said I was unqualified.

 *My grace is sufficient for you, for My power is made perfect in weakness.*

— 2 Corinthians 12:9

Esther's situation looked like a limitation. She was an orphan—no father, no mother—raised by her cousin Mordecai. She was a Jew living in exile under Persian rule, a minority with no political power. She was a woman in a male-dominated empire where queens could be discarded for disobedience. By natural reasoning, none of these circumstances suggested she could influence a king, much less save an entire nation.

I see myself and my story in Esther's story. It reminds me of the days before cell phones, when we took our film to the photo shop. First came the negatives. They had to be developed in a dark room. Those dark moments in your life are often the birthplace of purpose. Just because it started as a negative doesn't mean it can't become a beautiful image when fully developed.

What didn't kill you made you stronger. It doesn't have to end the way it began. Surround yourself with people who see what you can become—people who have your best interests at heart and who speak life into your future.

* * *

Chapter 2 Reflection

Personal Reflection

1. What challenges or "lemons" in your life have helped you grow?

_____

_____

_____

_____

_____

_____

_____

_____

2. How have pain, pressure, or unexpected circumstances shaped who you are becoming?

_____

_____

_____

_____

_____

_____

_____

3. In what areas are you still in the "negative" stage, waiting to be developed into something beautiful?

_____

_____

_____

_____

_____

_____

_____

Scripture Meditation

Meditate on the process of transformation. God uses every stage—even the dark moments—to prepare you for your purpose. After spending time with God and meditating on the Word below, write down anything He reveals to you. Be open and honest, despite any vulnerabilities.

> *Not only so, but we also glory in our sufferings, because we know that suffering produces perseverance; perseverance, character; and character, hope.*

> — Romans 5:3–4

_____
_____
_____
_____
_____
_____
_____
_____

Practical Action Step

Identify one area of your life where you are in a dark or challenging season. Pray and write down how God can turn that situation into growth, blessing, or transformation.

_____
_____
_____
_____
_____
_____
_____
_____

Chapter 3
Do You Know Your Family History?

Family reunions are so important. Beyond DNA, there's information you'll never find unless it is shared, spoken, or passed down. Every family needs a historian—both naturally and spiritually—to preserve the legacy.

I was young when my mother's sister passed away. I never got to know her personally, but I was told many times that I reminded others of her. In some way, that gave me a sense of connection, as if I wasn't alone, even without a personal reference or mentor.

I was still clueless. I was labeled. I tried to look different, to make the tone of my voice softer. I wanted to be like my older sister—just bubbly. I didn't understand. You just can't change your being. That was who I was. I could not change to fit in. And honestly, it was harder to pretend than to simply be me.

Then the word of the Lord came to me, saying: "Before I formed you in the womb I knew you; Before you were born I sanctified you; I ordained you a prophet to the nations."

Then said I: "Ah, Lord God! Behold, I cannot speak, for I am a youth."

But the Lord said to me: "Do not say, 'I am a youth,' For you shall go to all to whom I send you, And whatever I command you, you shall speak. Do not be afraid of their faces, For I am with you to deliver you," says the Lord.

Then the Lord put forth His hand and touched my mouth, and the Lord said to me: "Behold, I have put My words in your mouth.

See, I have this day set you over the nations and over the kingdoms, To root out and to pull down, To destroy and to throw down, To build and to plant."

— Jeremiah 1:4–9

Years later, at a family reunion on my dad's side, I discovered something remarkable: there were people in my family who operated in the gift of healing. It was in the family. I had experienced God's healing virtue several times in my own life, but I didn't realize it was part of a generational heritage. Unfortunately, it wasn't something that was openly talked about or nurtured, so I didn't pursue it deeply at the time. But now I can look back and see that God had been moving in my life for a long time, and what was in my family's history was also in me.

 Take with you seven pairs of every kind of clean animal, a male and its mate, and one pair of every kind of unclean animal, a male and its mate...

— Genesis 7:2–3

This passage reveals something powerful: God preserved both the clean and the unclean. And so it is with our history. There are family members whose stories we love to celebrate— the trailblazers, the praying grandmothers, the hard-working uncles. But there are also stories we avoid—the addictions, the abuse, the brokenness. Yet God does not discriminate. He can use anyone. He can take and make something beautiful out of your life.

He doesn't use you simply because you have an acronym behind your name or because you are the people's choice. God doesn't discard the unclean; He redeems it. He takes the good, the bad, and the hidden and repurposes it all for His glory. You are not disqualified because of your family's dysfunction. In fact, you are evidence that God's grace is generational.

Your family may be made up of many different pieces of the puzzle. It's the difference that makes the difference. Trace your history and identify what has been instrumental in shaping you. When you understand your family history—spiritually and naturally—you gain insight into both your battles and your blessings.

You learn what to break and what to build on. What you preserve, destroy, or rebuild determines the direction of generations after you. This is why it's so important to know your history—both naturally and spiritually. Just as I discovered in my own family, there are things in your bloodline that are worth celebrating and things that need breaking.

There may be a praying grandmother in your past, like Mordecai's faithful guidance in

Esther's life, or there may be patterns of pain and loss. But God uses it all. Esther's victory was tied to her heritage. She didn't abandon her identity to fit in at the palace; she preserved the faith of her people while stepping into a position of influence. She understood what to preserve, what to protect, and what to put to death. And that's the same calling we have—because what we choose to preserve, destroy, or rebuild will determine the direction of generations after us.

Chapter 3 Reflection

Personal Reflection

1. What truths about your family history have shaped who you are today?

_____

_____

_____

_____

_____

_____

_____

2. Are there patterns you need to break, or legacies you want to continue?

_____

_____

_____

_____

_____

_____

_____

3. How has God used your family—both the good and the difficult—to prepare you for your purpose?

_____

_____

_____

_____

_____

_____

Scripture Meditation

Reflect on your family history, acknowledging both the blessings and the brokenness. After spending time with God and meditating on the Word below, write down anything He reveals to you. Be open and honest, despite any vulnerabilities.

> *Remember the days of old; consider the generations long past. Ask your father and he will tell you, your elders, and they will explain to you.*
>
> — Deuteronomy 32:7

_____

_____

_____

_____

_____

_____

_____

_____

Practical Action Step

Write down three things from your family history that are worth preserving. Write down one pattern or legacy you want to intentionally break or transform. Then, lay before God to receive His divine wisdom regarding such.

_____

_____

_____

_____

_____

_____

_____

_____

_____

Part Two

Environment

Thriving in Unfamiliar Territory

The places we grow are not always the places we expect. Sometimes God places us in environments that feel uncomfortable, stretching, or unfamiliar—not to harm us, but to shape us. Esther thrived in a foreign palace, and you too can thrive where God has planted you. This section will help you find courage, faith, and resilience no matter your surroundings.

"When you pass through the waters, I will be with you; and when you pass through the rivers, they will not sweep over you." —Isaiah 43:2

Chapter 4
How Do You Thrive in New Surroundings?

Growing up in a male-dominated culture, I thought that was simply the way life was supposed to be. I didn't question it. I had no other expectations, and for a while, I was satisfied with the way things were.

But then I began to feel and experience things I could not control, things I didn't understand—and no one was there to explain them to me. I loved the Lord with all my heart. I was young, passionate, and believed what I had been told: *Go all the way with God. Catch on fire. The joy of the Lord is your strength.*

Yet when the Spirit of God began to move in me, I was silenced. I was told to sit down. It was embarrassing. I thought I was being obedient, yet I was shut down publicly. I wanted to be quiet after that, not to speak or testify again. It was devastating. It hurt deeply. Why? Because it felt like déjà vu.

I had been sat down once before, bound to the back bench. Yes—it was because of sin. I got pregnant out of wedlock. I repented. I was godly sorry, and I meant it. I loved God. After some years, I was reinstated back into service. Oh, how overjoyed I was! But now, this. Again?!

I was totally confused. Leadership had told me privately: *"I know the Lord uses you, and if I could get you on my side, that would be great."* Yet in public, I was humiliated.

Can you imagine how this played with my mind—and how emotionally and spiritually abandoned I felt? My confusion wasn't just because of what he had told me in private, but because of the way I wasn't seen as a member of his family, and as a woman. As if something was wrong with me.

And it made me question: *Well, what side are you on?* The pride. The manipulation. The customs and traditions of men.

My mother saw this happen to me more than once. She promised me that if it ever happened again, she would protect me. On the last occasion, my father intervened. He came and grabbed my hand—and in that moment, I felt what was in me flow down through my fingertips into his hand. I cried out, "My Dad got it! My Dad got it!" I didn't realize until later that what transferred was healing virtue.

That same week, my father was scheduled to have eye surgery on Friday. On Wednesday night, after that encounter, he received his healing. By Friday, when he went in for the procedure, the doctors found no trace of the problem. He no longer needed the operation.

Even though that miracle was powerful and beautiful, the experience leading up to it had crushed me. My heart and my mind were at war. I didn't want the Spirit to come upon me in that way anymore—not if it meant ridicule or misunderstanding. I was operating in an environment I wasn't accustomed to, and it left me shaken.

Later, I finally understood, and I had to debrief. I had to reconcile the pain of rejection with the truth of what God was doing through me.

You want to know how I made it? How I got through it? I prayed. I cried out to God. I had to strengthen myself in His Word. He became my best friend. I learned to trust what He said to me and to believe that He would bring me out.

I kept searching and searching for comfort and peace. My search took me to explore other churches. I would slip in and just sit quietly in the back. Sometimes I would travel with my kids and my sister—riding the bus in the rain—just to make it there. I did what I had to do to get to God.

Through it all I learned to trust in Jesus and to rely on God's Word. It became my rock and my refuge.

But in 2007, my father passed away—and I just lost it. After everything I had endured in the church, I had found courage to fight through. But losing my dad felt like too much. It was as if the last bit of strength inside me crumbled. I didn't want to get up. I didn't want to keep going. The pain felt deeper than words could carry. For a moment, I let despair silence me.

Then, one ordinary day, God broke through my darkness. I heard Him so clearly, so unmistakably, that it shook me to my core. He spoke and said: *"You will again be called My prophet."*

Those words pierced the silence of my sorrow. They carried me when I could not carry myself. They reminded me that my identity and calling were not defined by death, by rejection, or by the voices of others—but by the living Word of God.

That day something shifted. Grief didn't vanish, but hope returned. I realized God had not abandoned me. He was still writing my story.

From Orphan to Queen

Esther knew what it was to wrestle with fear and the unknown before stepping into boldness. She didn't have a perfect family history or a clear path laid out for her. She was an orphan, raised in exile, and hidden in a palace among strangers. Yet God used her precisely because she carried both the pain of loss and the strength of resilience.

Your story carries that same truth. You are not limited by what came before you. You don't have to follow old patterns or expectations. You can move forward and create something new. You may have heard of *Painting with a Twist*—but you hold your own paintbrush.

You have the power to create your own canvas. Your story is yours alone. It might look similar to someone else's, but it's not the same. People may see your glory, but they don't know the journey that brought you here. Sometimes you're expected to follow unspoken rules—to stay silent about your struggles, your healing, your growth. But those hidden places can be where deliverance happens. You've stepped into something new, something good, and you don't want to lose it.

But then come the hard questions:

- Do I stay quiet to keep the peace?
- Do I cover up what's wrong just to keep my position?
- Do I compromise my values for comfort?
- Do I sell out for a quick reward?

Or, maybe you were placed here for a reason. Not just to rise, but to help others rise. Maybe your promotion isn't just personal; it's purposeful. You were raised up to be a voice, an advocate, a light. So don't stay silent. Don't shrink back. Don't waste the opportunity. You were chosen to lead so that others can find rest, justice, and hope through you.

> *When the righteous are in authority, the people rejoice: but when the wicked beareth rule, the people mourn.*
>
> — Proverbs 29:2 (KJV)

Born Isabella Baumfree, Sojourner Truth chose to rename herself because she refused to carry the chains of her past into her future. She became *Sojourner*—a traveler on a journey—and *Truth*, because she was determined to declare the truth that sets captives free. Her name carried her mission, just like Esther's crown carried hers.

 *Don't sell your birthright! God will upset normal customs and hierarchies to advance His plan and purpose.*

— Genesis 25:29–34

Both Esther and Sojourner had to defy cultural expectations.

"Ain't I a woman? I have borne thirteen children, and seen most of them sold off to slavery. And when I cried out with my mother's grief, none but Jesus heard me! Ain't I a woman?"

— Sojourner Truth

Both Esther and Sojourner stood in the gap for others. Both proved that situation does not dictate destiny. Galatians 3:28 reminds us that we are not limited by labels, categories, or human divisions:

 *There is neither Jew nor Greek, there is neither bond nor free, there is neither male nor female: for ye are all one in Christ Jesus.*

— Galatians 3:28

John 8:32, 36 assures us that truth brings freedom:

 *Then you will know the truth, and the truth will set you free... So if the Son sets you free, you will be free indeed.*

— John 8:32, 36

Esther walked in that truth. *Sojourner* declared that truth.
And now... *I live in that truth.*

✶ ✶ ✶

Chapter 4 Reflection

Personal Reflection

1. Where have you felt silenced, overlooked, or shamed for your God-given gifts?

_____

_____

_____

_____

_____

_____

_____

_____

2. How can you step into your purpose despite fear or misunderstanding?

_____

_____

_____

_____

_____

_____

_____

_____

3. Who are the people God has placed around you to support and protect your calling?

_____

_____

_____

_____

_____

_____

_____

_____

Scripture Meditation

Meditate on the courage God provides to move beyond fear and into boldness. After spending time with God and meditating on the Word below, write down anything He reveals to you. Be open and honest, despite any vulnerabilities.

> *For God has not given us a spirit of fear, but of power and of love and of a sound mind.*

— 2 Timothy 1:7

_____
_____
_____
_____
_____
_____
_____
_____

Practical Action Step

Identify one area where fear or shame has held you back. Take one step this week to act in faith, whether it's speaking, sharing, or ministering boldly.

_____
_____
_____
_____
_____
_____
_____
_____
_____

Part Three

Mentorship

Learning, Growing, and Becoming

No one rises to their purpose alone. God sends mentors, guides, and spiritual voices to strengthen and prepare us for what lies ahead. Esther needed Mordecai's wisdom to step into her assignment—and you too are called to both receive and give mentorship. This section explores the power of guidance, impartation, and generational influence.

"Plans fail for lack of counsel, but with many advisers they succeed." —Proverbs 15:22

Chapter 5
Who's Mentoring You?

She still speaks. Precious memories. Oh, how they linger.

A woman of faith. A woman of great conviction and persuasion. A woman who defied the traditions of religion and the limits of nature. My mother was human, and she unapologetically expressed herself as such. She lived as God created her to live—without excuses—authentically, naturally, and spiritually. She modeled for me that holiness isn't about perfection; it's about integrity, faith, and courage to be who God called you to be.

I also honor Elder Johnnie Carolina, my pastor and father in the gospel, who once asked me: *"How are you going to teach anyone if you don't go through?"* That question has remained a guiding truth in my journey. Every test, every valley, every hardship—it has all become a part of my teaching, my testimony, and my ministry.

The wisdom of those who came before us is not meant to be forgotten. It is meant to be carried, lived, and passed on. Scripture affirms this in Titus 2:3–5, reminding us that older women are called to be teachers of good things—mentors who train the younger women in faith, family, discipline, and godly character.

My mother and my pastor embodied this truth. Their lives became living lessons of perseverance, holiness, and legacy. Their mentoring was not just in words—it was in how they lived, how they loved, and how they stood firm in their convictions.

Who is mentoring you? Who are the voices of wisdom that still linger in your heart? Mentorship is not just about instruction; it is about impartation. The legacy of those who walked before us gives us strength to walk into our future with courage and clarity.

Everybody needs a Mordecai. It may not be your biological parents. It may not be someone you expected. But as long as you have someone guiding you, pointing you in the right direction, and helping you stay on the straight and narrow path—you are blessed.

Mentors are God-sent. They help us see what we can't see. They challenge us, correct us, and speak life when we feel like giving up. Even Esther needed Mordecai to prepare her for her purpose.

I remember praying and asking God to send someone to speak into my son's life—specifically, a strong male role model. And God answered. He didn't send just one man; He sent multiple coaches who followed him through school and summer league, shaping him through their consistency, discipline, and encouragement.

It was a reminder: God hears our prayers. He cares about who's speaking into us—and into the next generation.

 And they rose early in the morning, and went forth into the wilderness of Tekoa: and as they went forth, Jehoshaphat stood and said, Hear me, O Judah, and ye inhabitants of Jerusalem; Believe in the Lord your God, so shall ye be established; believe his prophets, so shall ye prosper.

— 2 Chronicles 20:20 (KJV)

* * *

Chapter 5 Reflection

Personal Reflection

1. Who are the Mordecais in your life— those guiding, correcting, and mentoring you?

_____

_____

_____

_____

_____

_____

_____

2. How have mentors shaped your character, faith, and future?

_____

_____

_____

_____

_____

_____

_____

3. Are there areas where you need guidance or someone to help you see your potential?

_____

_____

_____

_____

_____

_____

_____

Scripture Meditation

Reflect on your family history, acknowledging both the blessings and the brokenness. After spending time with God and meditating on the Word below, write down anything He reveals to you. Be open and honest, despite any vulnerabilities.

"Older women likewise are to be reverent in behavior, not slanderers or slaves to much wine, teaching what is good, so that they may encourage the young women to love their husbands, to love their children, to be self-controlled, pure, working at home, kind, and submissive to their own husbands, that the word of God may not be reviled."

— Titus 2:3–5

_____

_____

_____

_____

_____

_____

_____

_____

Practical Action Step

Write the names of two or three people who have mentored you. Consider how you can receive their guidance more fully and apply it to your life this week.

_____

_____

_____

_____

_____

_____

_____

_____

Chapter 6
Are You a Parasite or a Protégé?

I am definitely a protégé! My desire to learn and grow didn't start with ambition or recognition, it started with love. I simply wanted to understand what was happening with my loved ones. Out of pure concern, I stepped into places I never thought I would go. And yet, God, in His divine wisdom, placed me in areas where I was able to go to school free of charge and gain the very knowledge I needed for my call.

At first, I didn't see it as preparation. I thought I was just doing what needed to be done. But the road I traveled was not easy. It required me to avail myself to the process, even when it meant walking through situations I didn't want to face. I had to feel things I didn't want to feel. I had to sit in spaces I didn't want to sit in. I was even classified with people I didn't want to be associated with. But through it all, God was teaching me. Through it all, I learned compassion. Through it all, I gained empathy. Through it all, I discovered the real meaning of love.

It was only after walking through affliction that I began to truly understand His Word:

> *It is good for me that I have been afflicted; that I might learn Thy statutes.*
>
> — Psalm 119:71

And I remember how God spoke to His people in the wilderness:

> *And thou shalt remember all the way which the Lord thy God led thee these*

forty years in the wilderness, to humble thee, and to prove thee, to know what was in thine heart, whether thou wouldest keep His commandments, or no.

— Deuteronomy 8:2

The wilderness is not wasted. Neither is affliction. Both are classrooms for those who are willing to be protégés. There's an old saying: *"Give me a fish, and I'll eat for a day. Teach me to fish, and I'll eat for a lifetime."* The difference between a parasite and a protégé is this: a parasite takes and consumes, while a protégé learns and grows.

I chose to be a protégé. And in the process, God was shaping not just my understanding, but my heart.

In Esther's story, Mordecai had to remind her: You didn't come into the palace just to play dress-up with your girlfriends. You were brought into the kingdom for such a time as this —not to simply enjoy the benefits, but to be used by God to save your people.

Sometimes we fall into situations that we didn't cause. It's not always our fault; it's just life. But that doesn't give us the right to take advantage of someone else's kindness. We are not called to exploit opportunity—we are called to rise with purpose.

Are you consuming or contributing? Some people are placed in your life not to serve you, but to guide you, to stretch you, and to bring out the best in you. And at some point, you must grow from being helped... to being a helper. From being covered to covering someone else. God is calling you out from under the wing so that you can become a mentor, a voice, a role model, a mouthpiece.

You may not realize it, but your obedience could carry the deliverance of a generation. Your "yes" could unlock freedom for a whole nation.

 *Blessed is the nation whose God is the Lord; and the people whom he hath chosen for his own inheritance.*

— Psalm 33:12 (KJV)

BJ Putnam's song *"Ask"* is a powerful reminder that we should ask God for the nations— not for control, but for healing, for revival, and for justice: *"One nation, under God, indivisible, with liberty and justice for all."* That's not just a pledge; it's a prayer for transformation.

 * * *

Chapter 6 Reflection

Personal Reflection

1. In your life, are you consuming more than contributing, or are you growing through the guidance and opportunities God provides?

_____

_____

_____

_____

_____

_____

_____

_____

2. How have challenges or afflictions shaped your understanding, compassion, and faith?

_____

_____

_____

_____

_____

_____

_____

_____

3. Who are you now in a position to mentor, help, or influence positively?

_____

_____

_____

_____

_____

_____

_____

_____

Scripture Meditation

Meditate on how affliction and guidance shape a protégé's heart for God's purpose. After spending time with God and meditating on the Word below, write down anything He reveals to you. Be open and honest, despite any vulnerabilities.

> *It is good for me that I have been afflicted, that I might learn your statutes.*
>
> — Psalm 119:71

> *And thou shalt remember all the way which the Lord thy God led thee these forty years in the wilderness, to humble thee, and to prove thee, to know what was in thine heart, whether thou wouldest keep his commandments, or no.*
>
> — Deuteronomy 8:2

_____

_____

_____

_____

_____

_____

_____

Practical Action Step

Identify one situation where you can choose to grow instead of just receive. Take one step this week to move from being helped to helping (i.e. mentoring, encouraging, or serving).

_____

_____

_____

_____

_____

_____

_____

Part Four

Positioning

Embracing Your Calling for Such a Time as This

There comes a time when you can no longer hide—you must rise into the place God has called you to. Positioning is not about titles or crowns; it is about stepping boldly into influence with faith, courage, and humility. Like Esther, you were chosen for such a time as this. This section is your call to walk fully in your royal identity and impact generations.

*"Who knows but that you have come to your royal position
for such a time as this?"* —Esther 4:14

Chapter 7
From Orphan to Queen

Insight is the capacity to gain an accurate and deep, intuitive understanding of a person or situation. It is the ability to have a clear, often sudden understanding of a complicated issue.

As in the game of chess, the queen must read the board and make her move—not just for herself, but for the greater good. One shift can change everything. One bold step can alter history. In the book of Esther, her cousin Mordecai asked her a life-defining question: *"What if you were brought into the kingdom for such a time as this?"*

Esther had to face the weight of responsibility. She could not stay hidden in the palace, enjoying her crown and the comforts of royalty. Lives were on the line. Her people's deliverance was in her mouth. She made a resolve that day: *"I will go to the king, even though it is against the law. And if I perish, I perish."* That kind of courage shifts destinies.

When God first called me into ministry, He told me something I didn't fully understand at the time: *"Do not worry about who accepts you, because they did not accept Me. And get up —or everything around you will go down."* I didn't realize then how much weight those words carried. At that time in my life, I was in hiding. I was broken. I was devastated. I wanted nothing more than to stay in bed, to let life pass me by. I remember people sitting around my bedside, watching me, waiting.

I had a choice: I could stay there, and everything connected to me would stay stuck too, or I could get up.

I got up. Not because I felt like it. Not because it was easy. But because I knew staying down meant everyone else would too. God reminded me, *"Don't mind the labels."* I didn't

41

understand back then what He meant. But now—in 2025—I see clearly. He told me from the beginning, *"I will bring it all together and sum it up."*

Today, I accept my position. I no longer see myself as an orphan. I walk as a queen. I walk in truth. And I share my story because perhaps someone else will hear it and be enlightened, set free, and empowered by it. I have officially moved from orphan to queen.

This shift is more than a title change. It is a complete transformation of identity, responsibility, and purpose. Esther understood this. She didn't step into her role blindly or carelessly. She knew what came before her. She knew what was at stake.

Queen Vashti lost her crown because she defied the king's command. Right or wrong, her refusal disrupted the cultural order and cost her everything. Esther entered the palace carrying the weight of that history. But instead of shrinking back in fear, she leaned into faith. She knew the risks. She knew the danger. But she also recognized the call. That's the essence of true queenship: insight + courage + faith.

To move from orphan to queen is to shift from survival to influence, from hidden pain to public purpose, from being covered to becoming a covering.

Here's your royal reminder:

> *"But you are a chosen people, a royal priesthood, a holy nation, God's special possession, that you may declare the praises of Him who called you out of darkness into His wonderful light."*

> — 1 Peter 2:9

You are *chosen*. You are *royal*. You are *called*.

✳ ✳ ✳

Chapter 7 Reflection

Personal Reflection

1. Esther made the choice to step out of hiding and into her purpose, even at great risk. Where in your life have you been tempted to stay hidden, silent, or small?

_____

_____

_____

_____

_____

_____

_____

2. Consider the words God spoke to the author: *"Get up—or everything around you will go down."* What might be connected to your obedience? Who could be waiting on your courage to rise?

_____

_____

_____

_____

_____

_____

_____

3. Reflect on your own journey. In what ways has God already shifted you from orphan thinking (feeling unworthy, rejected, or silenced) into queen thinking (walking in truth, purpose, and authority)?

_____

_____

_____

_____

_____

_____

Scripture Meditation

Pause and declare aloud: *"I am chosen. I am royal. I am God's possession. I have been called out of darkness into His light."* Then, imagine yourself stepping into Esther's shoes. What crown of responsibility and influence has God placed on your life? After spending time with God and meditating on the Word below, write down anything He reveals to you. Be open and honest, despite any vulnerabilities.

> *But you are a chosen people, a royal priesthood, a holy nation, God's special possession, that you may declare the praises of Him who called you out of darkness into His wonderful light.*
>
> — 1 Peter 2:9 (NIV)

_____

_____

_____

_____

_____

_____

_____

_____

_____

_____

_____

_____

_____

_____

_____

_____

_____

_____

_____

_____

_____

Practical Action Step

Write down one area of your life where you need to "get up" from discouragement, fear, or hiding. Identify at least one bold step you can take this week to walk in your royal identity. It might be speaking up, mentoring someone, sharing your testimony, or starting a project God placed on your heart.

_____

_____

_____

_____

_____

_____

_____

_____

_____

_____

_____

_____

_____

_____

_____

_____

_____

_____

_____

_____

Close out with a prayer of surrender, declaring:

"Lord, I will rise. I will step into my identity as Your daughter,
Your queen, for such a time as this."

Walk Into Your Royal Place

Every chapter of this journey has revealed one simple truth: *your situation does not dictate your future.* Through Esther's story, Sojourner Truth's example, your family's legacy, and even your own testimony, you have seen that God takes what looks like limitation and transforms it into destiny.

Like Esther, you may have started in obscurity—as an orphan, hidden and overlooked. But God always had a plan. He placed voices of mentorship in your life, He allowed your wilderness to shape you, and He gave you the courage to rise when everything in you wanted to stay hidden. And just like Esther, you are being positioned for such a time as this.

Your story is proof that:

- You are not disqualified by your past
- You are not limited by labels or expectations
- You are not forgotten by God

Instead, you are:

- A battle axe in the hand of the Lord (Jeremiah 51:20)
- A chosen generation, a royal priesthood (1 Peter 2:9)
- A woman who has shifted from orphan to queen—called to use her voice, her influence, and her testimony to bring freedom to others

Final Encouragement

You may not always understand the process. Some days may feel like negatives in the darkroom. But remember: negatives are where the picture begins to form. When developed by the Master's hand, your life becomes a beautiful image of His glory.

- Don't despise the affliction; it taught you His statutes.
- Don't resent the wilderness; it humbled you and proved your heart.
- Don't fear the crown; it is not a weight of luxury, but a mantle of responsibility.
- You are a protégé who has become a mentor.
- You are no longer silent; you are a voice.
- You are no longer hidden; you are chosen.
- You are no longer an orphan; you are a queen.

A Prayer of Release: The Serenity Prayer

God, grant me the serenity
To accept the things I cannot change,
The courage to change the things I can,
And the wisdom to know the difference.

Glossary of Truth

Words carry weight. Throughout this workbook, certain terms have been repeated and emphasized because they shape our understanding of identity, purpose, and calling. To ensure clarity, and to invite you deeper into their meaning, this section provides definitions of key words used in the journey from *orphan to queen*.

Some of these vocabulary words are biblical terms, while others are everyday words that have been given new life through spiritual insight. Together, they form a glossary of truth, reminders that language has the power to shape how we see ourselves, our God, and our destiny.

* * *

- *Orphan*: A child whose parents are deceased, or one deprived of parental care, support, or supervision.

- *Care:* The provision of what is necessary for health, welfare, maintenance, and protection. Serious attention and concern.

- *Remnant*: A small remaining quantity of something; leftovers, residue. A piece of fabric left after the rest has been used or sold. A surviving trace or vestige.

- *Vestige:* A trace or mark of something that is disappearing or no longer exists.

Glossary of Truth

- *Exile*: The state of being sent away or kept from one's homeland, often for political reasons; a forced migration. For followers of Christ, exile also has a spiritual meaning: living in a land, influenced by a culture, among a people that are not your own.

- *Parasite*: A person who habitually relies on or exploits others while giving nothing in return; one who takes advantage of another.

- *Protégé*: A person guided and supported by someone older, more experienced, or influential. One under the patronage, protection, or care of someone invested in their growth and success.

- *Queen*: A woman who embraces the best version of herself. She speaks with kindness and love to herself and to others. A queen has shed self-limiting beliefs and walks in freedom, influence, and authority. She is both a royal lady and a visionary leader.

- *Queen* (*Chess Piece*): The most powerful chess piece, able to move any number of unobstructed squares in any direction along a rank, file, or diagonal. Symbolically, the queen represents strategy, influence, and authority.

Acknowledgments

First and foremost, I want to thank my Lord and Savior, Jesus Christ, for allowing me to make it this far and to share my story.

To my husband, Eric Barron: thank you for all the daily life lessons and for challenging me to make my calling and election sure.

To my children—Erica, Eikeem, and Tiera: you were born in and through my metamorphosis. You hung in there. May God bless you!

To Apostle F.L. Person and Bishop Derric Wright: thank you for your continued support and for pouring into me on this journey.

To my sisters—Jackie Wright, Darlene Wright, Naurette Hill, and Janet Harper: thank you for your support and prayers during the worst of times. Nothing shall be wasted.

To my trusted voices—Apostle Roberta Cutright, Pastor Patricia Lampkin, and my special friend Staci Harrison: thank you for the push.

About the Author

Gail Wright-Barron, a native of Philadelphia, PA, is a devoted wife to Eric Barron and mother to her three children—Erica, Eikeem, and Tiera. She grew up faithfully attending her family's ministry, The New Creation, where her foundation in faith was formed. Gail is one of six children born to the late Thomas and Lessie Wright.

From childhood, Gail experienced the undeniable power of God moving in her life—even when she lacked the words to express it. Though she was often silenced in church and never formally trained in her gifting, her journey through life, motherhood, and reconciliation in marriage became the classroom where the Lord revealed her true identity and nurtured her calling.

Drawing inspiration from the story of Esther and her own personal testimony, Gail conveys a powerful message of hope. Her heart is to encourage women to remain committed to the path God has set before them, no matter the challenges. She is passionately dedicated to helping women discover their authentic identity in Christ—just as she has discovered her own.

www.ingramcontent.com/pod-product-compliance
Lightning Source LLC
Chambersburg PA
CBHW040512150626
46551CB00030B/2506